VOGUE KNITTING

WEEKEND
KNITS

on the go!™

VOGUE KNITTING

# WEEKEND KNITS

SIXTH&SPRING BOOKS
NEW YORK

SIXTH&SPRING BOOKS
233 Spring Street
New York, New York 10013

Library of Congress Cataloging-in-Publication Data

Weekend knits.
     p. cm. -- (Vogue knitting on the go!)
     ISBN 1-931543-23-2
     1. Knitting--Patterns. I. Series.

     TT825 .W44 2003
     746.43'20432--dc21                                    2002030407

Manufactured in China

1 3 5 7 9 10 8 6 4 2

First Edition

# TABLE OF CONTENTS

# INTRODUCTION

Juggling careers, families and demanding schedules often leaves us with little spare time. What better way to use these precious free moments than to tackle a quick and easy knitting project? *Weekend Knits* presents twenty-one basic yet sophisticated projects that are appropriate for knitters of any skill level.

Each of the projects, including those with colorwork and cable designs, are deceptively simple to knit. From a *Mohair Cardigan*, a *Cable-Knit Belt* or wee *Cap and Booties*, each project has been carefully designed and requires minimal shaping and finishing techniques so you can create a portable, no-fuss design in 48 hours or less.

Offered in an array of luxurious fibers and exquisite colors, the projects are as easy to knit as they are fun to wear. Even inexperienced knitters can start a fabulous faux-fur *Tank Top* on Thursday and wear it to a party on Saturday evening. Maximize commuting time by fashioning a snazzy *Baby Blanket* for a weekend baby shower, or stitch up a pair of *Seed-Stitch Mittens* and wear them to work the next day.

The patterns serve as blank canvases, so we encourage you to experiment with yarns, colors and embellishments and let your imagination take over. Windows of opportunity abound to squeeze in a row or two here and there, adding up to a completed garment or accessory in no time. So before you step out the door, grab your yarn and needles, make room in your tote for your stitching—and get ready to **KNIT ON THE GO!**

# THE BASICS

Hand-knits are everywhere—from the covers of fashion magazines and the runways of Paris, Milan and New York, to the shelves of the most exclusive boutiques. With a renewed interest in knitwear comes the desire to create unique hand-knits of one's own. The enormous appeal of a hand-knit garment or accessory stitched in luscious yarns has encouraged knitters past and present, novice and experienced, to pick up their needles and reacquaint themselves with this age-old craft.

Small, simple projects are ideal for experimenting with new stitch patterns, testing out new techniques or improving your skills. *Weekend Knits* offers more than twenty striking designs, with each project requiring no more than forty-eight hours to complete. Simply cast on Saturday and wear it Monday.

No-fuss knitting doesn't mean you have to sacrifice style for speed. Stitched in the latest yarns and requiring minimal finishing, the projects are ideally suited for knitters of all skill levels. So whether you're a beginner knitter picking up needles for the first time or a more experienced stitcher looking for a quick-knit project to fly through over a weekend, you'll fine just what you're looking for. An invitation to a party next Saturday night is an invitation to knit something fabulous, like the faux-fur "Tank Top" on page 18; or try the sensuously silken "Cabled Sleeveless Shell" on page 50. If a gift for an expectant friend is on your shopping list, try the precious variegated bouclé "Toddler's Cardigan" on page 20, or wrap a little one in a lovely "Baby Blanket" on page 26. Don't forget your better half with the "Man's Weekend Sweater" on page 71. Even quick accessories from hats to socks to scarves are included.

## SIZING

When determining what size to make, be sure to consult the "Knitted Measurements" section of each pattern, as well as the schematic drawings. Measure a sweater that fits you well to decide which size is best for you.

## YARN SELECTION

For an exact reproduction of the projects photographed, use the yarn listed in the "Materials" section of the pattern. We've chosen yarns that are readily available in the U.S. and Canada at the time of printing. The Resources list on pages 78 and 79 provides addresses of yarn distributors. Contact them for the name of a retailer in your area.

## YARN SUBSTITUTION

You may wish to substitute yarns. Perhaps you view small-scale projects as a chance to incorporate leftovers from your yarn stash, or maybe the yarn specified is not available in your area. You'll need to knit to the given gauge to obtain the knitted measurements with a substitute yarn (see "Gauge" on page 11). Be sure to consider

## GAUGE

It is always important to knit a gauge swatch, and it is even more so with garments to ensure proper fit.

Patterns usually state gauge over a 4"/10cm span, however it's beneficial to make a larger test swatch. This gives a more precise stitch gauge, a better idea of the appearance and drape of the knitted fabric, and gives you a chance to familiarize yourself with the stitch pattern.

The type of needles used—straight- or double-pointed, wood or metal—will influence gauge, so knit your swatch with the needles you plan to use for the project. Measure gauge as illustrated. Try different needle sizes until your sample measures the required number of stitches and rows. *To get fewer stitches to the inch/cm, use larger needles; to get more stitches to the inch/cm, use smaller needles.*

Knitting in the round may tighten the gauge, so if you measured the gauge on a flat swatch, take another gauge reading after you begin knitting. When the piece measures at least 2"/5cm, lay it flat and measure over the stitches in the center of the piece, as the side stitches may be distorted.

It's a good idea to keep your gauge swatch in order to test blocking and cleaning methods.

how the fiber content of the substitute yarn will affect the comfort and ease of care of your projects.

To facilitate yarn substitution, *Vogue Knitting* grades yarn by the standard stitch gauge obtained in stockinette stitch. You'll find a grading number in the "Materials" section of the pattern, immediately following the fiber type of the yarn. Look for a substitute yarn that falls in the same category. The suggested needle size and gauge on the ball band should be comparable to that on the Yarn Symbols chart (see page 13).

After you've successfully gauge-swatched a yarn, you'll need to figure out how much of the substitute yarn the project requires. First, find the total length of the original yarn in the pattern (multiply number of balls by yards/meters per ball). Divide this figure by the new yards/meters per ball (listed on the ball band). Round up to the next whole number. The answer is the number of balls required.

## FOLLOWING CHARTS

Charts are a convenient way to follow color work, lace, cable and other stitch patterns at a glance. *Vogue Knitting* stitch charts utilize the universal knitting language of "symbolcraft." When knitting back and forth in rows, read charts from right to left on right-side (RS) rows and from left to right on wrong-side (WS) rows, repeating any stitch and row repeats as directed in the pattern. When knitting in the round, read charts from right to left on every round. Posting a self-adhesive note under your working row is an easy way to keep track of your place on a chart.

## BLOCKING

Blocking is an all-important finishing step in the knitting process. It is the best way to shape pattern pieces and smooth knitted edges in preparation for sewing together. Most garments retain their shape if the blocking stages in the instructions are followed carefully. Choose a blocking method according to the yarn care label. When in doubt, test-block your gauge swatch.

### WET BLOCK METHOD

Using rust-proof pins, pin pieces to measurements on a flat surface and lightly dampen using a spray bottle. Allow to dry before removing pins.

### STEAM BLOCK METHOD

With WS facing, pin pieces. Steam lightly, holding the iron 2"/5cm above the knitting. Do not press or it will flatten the stitches.

## FINISHING

The pieces in this book use a variety of finishing techniques, from crocheting around the edges to knitting the shoulder seams together to embroidering the edges. Many of the garments have self-finished edges, meaning there are no added borders to the outside edges. Once you have finished knitting the pieces and have sewn them together, you are done.

### SEWING

When using a very bulky or highly textured yarn, it is sometimes easier to seam pieces together with a finer, flat yarn. Just be sure that your sewing yarn closely matches the original yarn used in your project in color and washability.

### CARE

Refer to the yarn label for the recommended cleaning method. Many of the projects in the book can be either washed by hand or in the machine on a gentle or wool cycle, in lukewarm water with a mild detergent. Do not agitate or soak for more than ten minutes. Rinse gently with tepid water, fold in a towel and gently press the water out. Lay flat to dry away from excess heat and light. Check the yarn band for any specific care instructions such as dry cleaning or tumble drying.

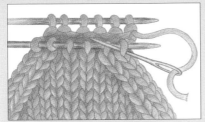

**1** Insert tapestry needle purlwise (as shown) through first stitch on front needle. Pull yarn through, leaving that stitch on knitting needle.

**2** Insert tapestry needle knitwise (as shown) through first stitch on back needle. Pull yarn through, leaving stitch on knitting needle.

**3** Insert tapestry needle knitwise through first stitch on front needle, slip stitch off needle and insert tapestry needle purlwise (as shown) through next stitch on front needle. Pull yarn through, leaving this stitch on needle.

**4** Insert tapestry needle purlwise through first stitch on back needle. Slip stitch off needle and insert tapestry needle knitwise (as shown) through next stitch on back needle. Pull yarn through, leaving this stitch on needle. Repeat steps 3 and 4 until all stitches on both front and back needles have been grafted. Fasten off and weave in end.

## YARN SYMBOLS

① **Fine Weight**
(29-32 stitches per 4"/10cm)
*Includes baby and fingering yarns and some of the heavier crochet cottons. The range of needle sizes is 0-4 (2-3.5mm).*

② **Lightweight**
(25-28 stitches per 4"/10cm)
*Includes sport yarn, sock yarn, UK 4-ply and lightweight DK yarns. The range of needle sizes is 3-6 (3.25-4mm).*

③ **Medium Weight**
(21-24 stitches per 4"/10cm)
*Includes DK and worsted, the most commonly used knitting yarns. The range of needle sizes is 6-9 (4-5.5mm).*

④ **Medium-heavy Weight**
(17-20 stitches per 4"/10cm)
*Also called heavy worsted or Aran. The range of needle sizes is 8-10 (5-6mm).*

⑤ **Bulky Weight**
(13-16 stitches per 4"/10cm)
*Also called chunky. Includes heavier Icelandic yarns. The range of needle sizes is 10-11 (6-8mm).*

⑥ **Extra-bulky Weight**
(9-12 stitches per 4"/10cm)
*The heaviest yarns available. The range of needle sizes is 11 and up (8mm and up).*

# CROCHET STITCHES

### CHAIN

**1** Pass the yarn over the hook and catch it with the hook.

**2** Draw the yarn through the loop on the hook.

**3** Repeat steps 1 and 2 to make a chain.

### SINGLE CROCHET

**1** Insert the hook through top two loops of a stitch. Pass the yarn over the hook and draw up a loop—two loops on hook.

**2** Pass the yarn over the hook and draw through both loops on hook.

**3** Continue in the same way, inserting the hook into each stitch.

### HALF-DOUBLE CROCHET

**1** Pass the yarn over the hook. Insert the hook through the top two loops of a stitch.

**2** Pass the yarn over the hook and draw up a loop—three loops on hook. Pass the yarn over the hook.

**3** Draw through all three loops on hook.

### DOUBLE CROCHET

**1** Pass the yarn over the hook. Insert the hook through the top two loops of a stitch.

**2** Pass the yarn over the hook and draw up a loop— three loops on hook.

**3** Pass the yarn over the hook and draw it through the first two loops on the hook, pass the yarn over the hook and draw through the remaining two loops. Continue in the same way, inserting the hook into each stitch.

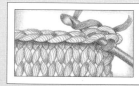

### SLIP STITCH

Insert the crochet hook into a stitch, catch the yarn and pull up a loop. Draw the loop through the loop on the hook.

Illustrations: Joni Coniglio

## TO BEGIN SEAMING

If you have left a long tail from your cast-on row, you can use this strand to begin sewing. To make a neat join at the lower edge with no gap, use the technique shown here. Thread the strand into a yarn needle. With the rights sides of both pieces facing you, insert the yarn needle from back to front into the corner stitch of the piece without the tail. Making a figure eight with the yarn, insert the needle from back to front into the stitch with the cast-on tail. Tighten to close the gap.

## INVISIBLE SEAMING: STOCKINETTE ST

To make an invisible side seam in a garment worked in stockinette stitch, insert the tapestry needle under the horizontal bar between the first and second stitches. Insert the needle into the corresponding bar on the other piece. Pull the yarn gently until the sides meet. Continue alternating from side to side.

## THREE-NEEDLE BIND-OFF

**1** With RS placed together, hold pieces on two parallel needles. Insert a third needle knitwise into the first stitch of each needle, and wrap the yarn around the needle as if to knit.

**2** Knit these two stitches together, and slip them off the needles. *Knit the next two stitches together in the same manner.

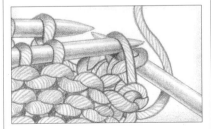

**3** Slip the first stitch on the third needle over the second stitch and off the needle. Repeat from the * in Step 2 across the row until all stitches have been bound off.

## POMPOMS

**1** Following the template, cut two circular pieces of cardboard.

**2** Hold the two circles together and wrap the yarn tightly around the cardboard several times. Secure and carefully cut the yarn.

**3** Tie a piece of yarn tightly between the two circles. Remove the cardboard and trim the pompom to the desired size.

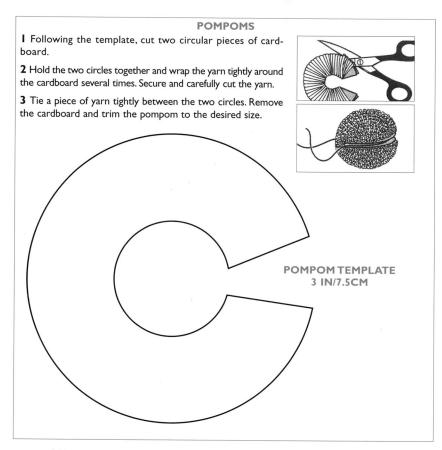

POMPOM TEMPLATE
3 IN/7.5CM

# KNITTING TERMS AND ABBREVIATIONS

**approx** approximately

**beg** begin(ning)

**bind off** Used to finish an edge and keep stitches from unraveling. Lift the first stitch over the second, the second over the third, etc. (UK: cast off)

**cast on** A foundation row of stitches placed on the needle in order to begin knitting.

**CC** contrast color

**ch** chain(s)

**cm** centimeter(s)

**cont** continue(ing)

**dc** double crochet (UK: tr-treble)

**dec** decrease(ing)–Reduce the stitches in a row (knit 2 together).

**dpn** double-pointed needle(s)

**foll** follow(s)(ing)

**g** gram(s)

**garter stitch** Knit every row. Circular knitting: knit one round, then purl one round.

**hdc** half double crochet (UK: htr-half treble)

**inc** increase(ing)–Add stitches in a row (knit into the front and back of a stitch).

**k** knit

**k2tog** knit 2 stitches together

**LH** left-hand

**lp(s)** loop(s)

**m** meter(s)

**M1** make one stitch–With the needle tip, lift the strand between last stitch worked and next stitch on the left-hand needle and knit into the back of it. One stitch has been added.

**MC** main color

**mm** millimeter(s)

**no stitch** On some charts, "no stitch" is indicated with shaded spaces where stitches have been decreased or not yet made. In such cases, work the stitches of the chart, skipping over the "no stitch" spaces.

**oz** ounce(s)

**p** purl

**p2tog** purl 2 stitches together

**pat(s)** pattern

**pick up and knit (purl)** Knit (or purl) into the loops along an edge.

**pm** place markers–Place or attach a loop of contrast yarn or purchased stitch marker as indicated.

**psso** pass slip stitch(es) over

**rem** remain(s)(ing)

**rep** repeat

**rev St st** reverse stockinette stitch–Purl right-side rows, knit wrong-side rows. Circular knitting: purl all rounds. (UK: reverse stocking stitch)

**rnd(s)** round(s)

**RH** right-hand

**RS** right side(s)

**sc** single crochet (UK: dc-double crochet)

**sk** skip

**SKP** Slip 1, knit 1, pass slip stitch over knit 1.

**SK2P** Slip 1, knit 2 together, pass slip stitch over the knit 2 together.

**sl** slip–An unworked stitch made by passing a stitch from the left-hand to the right-hand needle as if to purl.

**sl st** slip stitch (UK: single crochet)

**ssk** slip, slip, knit–Slip next 2 stitches knitwise, one at a time, to right-hand needle. Insert tip of left-hand needle into fronts of these stitches from left to right. Knit them together. One stitch has been decreased.

**sssk** Slip next 3 sts knitwise, one at a time, to right-hand needle. Insert tip of left-hand needle into fronts of these stitches from left to right. Knit them together. Two stitches have been decreased.

**st(s)** stitch(es)

**St st** Stockinette stitch–Knit right-side rows, purl wrong-side rows. Circular knitting: knit all rounds. (UK: stocking stitch)

**tbl** through back of loop

**tog** together

**WS** wrong side(s)

**wyib** with yarn in back

**wyif** with yarn in front

**work even** Continue in pattern without increasing or decreasing. (UK: work straight)

**yd** yard(s)

**yo** yarn over–Make a new stitch by wrapping the yarn over the right-hand needle. (UK: yfwd, yon, yrn)

**\*** = repeat directions following * as many times as indicated.

**[ ]** = Repeat directions inside brackets as many times as indicated.

*Fur sure*

**Dressed up or dressed down, this versatile top can be worn for any occasion. The soft furry yarn makes it comfortable against the skin. Designed by Judy Nemish.**

### SIZES

Instructions are written for size X-Small. Changes for Small, Medium and Large are in parentheses.

### KNITTED MEASUREMENTS

- Bust 32 (35, 38, 41)"/81 (89, 96.5, 104)cm
- Length 21 (21¾, 22½, 23)"/53 (55, 57, 58.5)cm

### MATERIALS

- 3 (3, 4, 5) 4oz/125g skeins (each approx 200yd/180m) of Cherry Hill Tree Yarns *Ballerina Mini* (wool ④) in blueberry hill
- One pair size 7 (4.5mm) needles *or size to obtain gauge*
- Size E/4 (3.5mm) crochet hook

### GAUGE

18 sts and 28 rows to 4"/10cm over St st using size 7 (4.5mm) needles.
*Take time to check gauge.*

### BACK

Cast on 73 (79, 87, 93) sts. Work in St st until piece measures 13"/33cm from beg, end with a WS row.

### Armhole shaping

**Next (dec) row (RS)** K1, SSK, k to last 3 sts, k2tog, k1. Work 1 row even. Rep last 2 rows 15 (19, 22, 24) times more, then work dec row every 4th row 1 (0, 0, 0) time—39 (39, 41, 43) sts.

### Neck shaping

**Next row (RS)** Work 12 sts, join a 2nd ball of yarn and bind off center 15 (15, 17, 19) sts, work to end. Working both sides at once, bind off from each neck edge 2 sts 3 times, 1 st 3 times—3 sts. Work even in St st until straps measure 3"/7.5cm. Bind off.

### FRONT

Work same as for back.

### FINISHING

Block pieces to measurements. Sew shoulder and side seams. With RS facing and crochet hook, work 1 row sc around neck and lower edge.

8½ (8½, 9, 9½)"

3"

21 (21¾, 22½, 23)"

FRONT & BACK

5 (5¾, 6½, 7)"

13"

16 (17½, 19, 20½)"

# TODDLER'S CARDIGAN

*Pocket full of posies*

*Very Easy Very Vogue*

**The perfect gift that knits up in a jiffy. Variegated bouclé adds touchable texture—this one is sure to be passed on from generation to generation. Designed by Jean Guirguis.**

## SIZES
Instructions are written for size 12 months. Changes for 18 and 24 months are in parentheses.

## KNITTED MEASUREMENTS
■ Chest (buttoned) 24 (26, 28½)"/61 (66, 72.5)cm
■ Length 11 (11½, 12)"/28 (29, 30.5)cm
■ Upper arm 9 (10, 11)"/23 (25.5, 28)cm

## MATERIALS
■ 4 (5, 6) 1¾oz/50g skeins (each approx 162yd/150m) of Wendy *Rembrandt* (wool ④) in #3503 pink
■ One pair size 9 (5.5mm) needles *or size to obtain gauge*
■ Stitch holders and markers
■ Five ½"/13mm buttons
■ Dried or artificial flowers (optional)

## GAUGE
14 sts and 16 rows to 4"/10cm over St st using size 9 (5.5mm) needles and 2 strands held tog.
*Take time to check gauge.*

## NOTE
Use 2 strands of yarn held tog throughout.

## BACK
With 2 strands held tog, cast on 40 (44, 48) sts. Work in k1, p1 rib for 1"/2.5cm. Work in St st until piece measures 11 (11½, 12)"/28 (29, 30.5)cm from beg. Bind off all sts.

## POCKET LININGS
(make 2)
With 2 strands held tog, cast on 11 sts. Work in St st for 2½"/6.5cm. Sl sts to holder.

## LEFT FRONT
With 2 strands held tog, cast on 23 (25, 27) sts. Work in k1, p1 rib for 1"/2.5cm, end with a WS row.

**Next row (RS)** Work in St st to last 2 sts p1, k1. Cont as established, working 2 front edge sts in rib, until piece measures 3½"/9cm from beg, end with a WS row.

**Pocket joining**

**Next row (RS)** Work 5 (7, 9) sts, sl next 11 sts to holder, work to end.

**Next row** Work 7 sts, work across 11 sts of one pocket lining, work to end. Work even until piece measures 9 (9½, 10)"/23 (24, 25.5)cm from beg, end with a RS row.

**Neck shaping**

**Next row (WS)** Bind off 4 sts (neck edge), work to end. Cont to bind off 3 sts from neck edge 3 times. Bind off rem 10 (12, 14) sts for shoulder. Place markers on front edge for 4 buttons, the first one ½"/1.5cm from lower edge, the last one

2"/5cm below neck shaping and 2 spaced evenly between.

## RIGHT FRONT
Work to correspond to left front, reversing all shaping and working 4 buttonholes in front rib edge as foll: K1, k2tog, yo.

## SLEEVES
With 2 strands held tog, cast on 18 sts. Work in k1, p1 rib for 1"/2.5cm. Work in St st, inc 1 st each side every other row 7 (9, 5) times, every 0 (0, 4th) row 0 (0, 5) times—32 (36, 38) sts. Work even until piece measures 6 (6½, 9½)"/15 (16.5, 24)cm from beg. Bind off.

## FINISHING
Block pieces to measurement. Sew shoulder seams.

### Neckband
With RS facing, pick up and k42 sts evenly around neck edge. Work in k1, p1 rib for ½"/1.5cm. On next row, work buttonhole on right front as before. Cont in rib until neckband measures 1"/2.5cm. Bind off in rib.

### Pocket borders
Sl 11 sts from holder to needle and work in k1, p1 rib for 1"/2.5cm. Bind off in rib.

Sew sides of rib borders in place. Sew pocket linings in place on WS.

Place markers 4½ (5, 5½)"/11.5 (12.5, 14)cm down from each shoulder edge. Sew in sleeves between markers. Sew side and sleeve seams. Sew on buttons. If desired, tack down flowers in pocket.

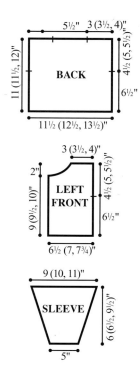

BACK

5½"  3 (3½, 4)"

11 (11½, 12)"

4½ (5, 5½)"

6½"

11½ (12½, 13½)"

LEFT FRONT

3 (3½, 4)"

2"

9 (9½, 10)"

4½ (5, 5½)"

6½"

6½ (7, 7¾)"

SLEEVE

9 (10, 11)"

6 (6½, 9½)"

5"

# CROPPED CARDIGAN

*Romancing the ribbon*

**Lighter than air, this silk top is a breeze to knit. Alternate two rows of Rippins with one row of Ribbons in an easy textured stitch pattern for a daytime or evening look. Designed by Hanah Exley of Hanah Silk.**

## SIZES

Instructions are written for size Small. Changes for Medium are in parentheses.

## KNITTED MEASUREMENTS

- Bust (closed) 30 (32)"/76 (81)cm
- Length 15 (16½)"/38 (42)cm

## MATERIALS

- 100 (120) yards of Hanah Silk *Rippins* (silk ⑥) (A)
- 2 (3) spools of Hanah Silk *Ribbons* (silk ⑥) (B)
- Size 19 (16mm) circular needles, 24"/60cm long *or size to obtain gauge*
- Size H/8 (5mm) crochet hook

## GAUGE

7 sts and 11 rows to 4"/10cm over stripe pat using size 19 (16mm) needles.
*Take time to check gauge.*

## NOTES

**Hints about knitting with Rippins**
The crinkled silk comes packaged in five 10yd strips. Remove the strips carefully one at a time and make butterflies (The silk will shed strings. Pull them off as you make the butterflies). To make a butterfly, wind the silk around 4 fingers to the last 15"/38cm. Wrap this around the middle and pull the last bit through to hold. Pull the starting end as you need the ribbon. Tie the butterflies together, as you need them, with a square knot (right over left and under, left over right and under).

**Hints about knitting with Ribbons**
Pull all the silk from the spools, cutting out the joins as you go. Tie them together as you need them.

## STRIPE PATTERN

**Row 1 (RS)** With B, knit. Do not turn work. Slide sts back to beg of needle to work next row from RS.
**Row 2 (RS)** With A, knit. Turn.
**Row 3 (WS)** With B, knit. Turn.
**Row 4 (RS)** With B, knit. Turn.
**Row 5 (WS)** With A, purl. Do not turn work. Slide sts to beg of needle to work next row from WS.
**Row 6 (WS)** With B, knit. Turn.
Rep rows 1-6 for stripe pat.

## BACK

With A, cast on 26 (28) sts. Work in stripe pat for 8 (9)"/20.5 (23)cm.

## SLEEVES

Cont in stripe pat, cast on 3 sts at beg of next 2 rows. Inc 1 st each side every other row 5 times—42 (44) sts. Work even until armhole measures 4½ (5)"/11.5 (12.5)cm from cast-on. Bind off 2 sts at beg of next 6 rows—30 (32) sts. Bind off.

## LEFT FRONT

With A, cast on 13 (14) sts. Work as for back, shaping armhole and shoulder at side edge (beg of RS rows) only.

## RIGHT FRONT

Work as for left front, reversing shaping.

## FINISHING

Spray pieces lightly with water, pull into shape and let dry. Match up shoulders and decide on neckline width. Sew shoulder and side seams. With RS facing, crochet hook and B, work sc evenly along right front edge, do not turn and working from left to right work backwards sc. Work in same way along left front. Lightly steam piece.

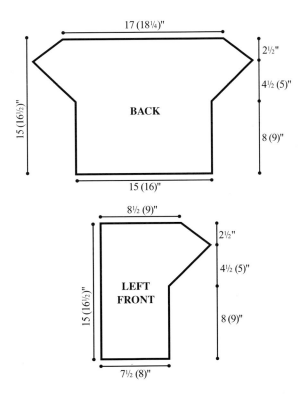

Your wee one will be warm and comfy under this colorful cotton blankie designed by Margarita Mejia. Varying stripes provide visual impact and the scalloped crocheted edge adds the perfect finishing touch.

## KNITTED MEASUREMENTS

■ 25" x 21½"/63.5 x 54.5cm

## MATERIALS

■ 1 1¾oz/50g skeins (each approx 84yd/77m) of Mission Falls/Unique Kolours *1824 Cotton* (cotton ④) each in #404 navy (A), #403 med blue (B), #303 blue/green (C), #302 olive green (D), #203 fuchsia (E), #407 purple (F), #204 gold (G) and #402 seafoam green (H)

■ One pair size 6 (4mm) needles *or size to obtain gauge*

■ Size G/6 (4.5mm) crochet hook

## GAUGE

18 sts and 36 rows to 4"/10cm over garter st using size 6 (4mm) needles.
*Take time to check gauge.*

## BLANKET

### Panel I

With D, cast on 28 sts. Working in garter st, work 24 rows each D, A, E, C, G, B, F, H. Bind off.

### Panel 2

With H, cast on 28 sts. Working in garter st, work 8 rows each H, A, E, G, C, F, B, D, G, A, H, E, B, F, D, C, A, G, B, E, H, D, F, C. Bind off.

### Panel 3

With B, cast on 28 sts. Working in garter st, work 32 rows each B, E, C, A, D, G. Bind off.

### Panel 4

With G, cast on 28 sts. Working in garter st, work 16 rows each G, F, C, B, A, D, E, H, G, B, F, E. Bind off.

## FINISHING

Block panels and sew tog.

### Border

**Rnd I** With RS facing, crochet hook and A, work sc and ch 1 evenly around outside edges, working sc, ch 2, sc in each corner.

**Rnd 2** With C, work 2 dc, ch 3 and 2 dc in each ch-1 sp, working [2 dc, ch 3] twice, 2 dc in each corner ch-2 sp. **Rnd 3** With G, work 2 sc, ch 2, 2 sc in each ch-3 sp.

# GIRL'S EASY PULLOVER

*Play mate*

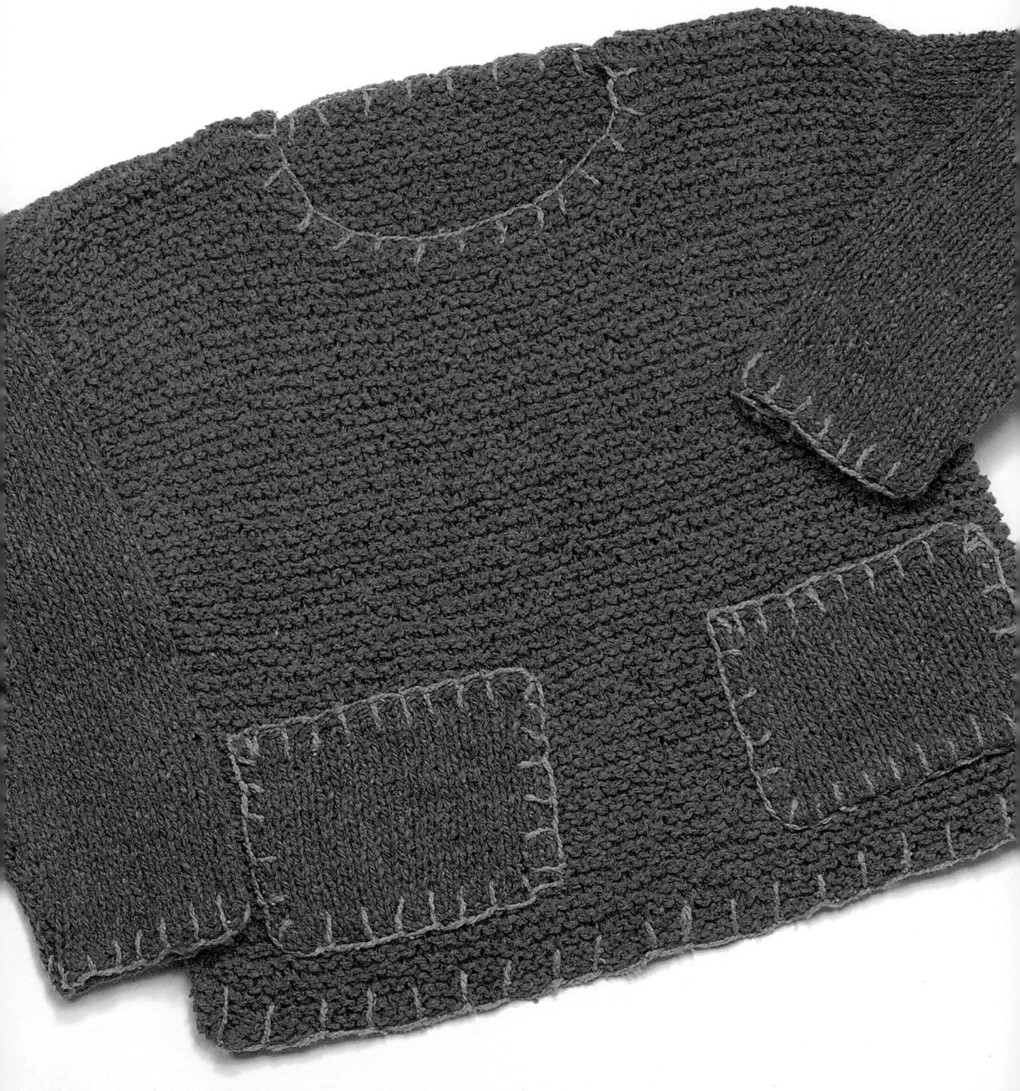

**A mix of garter and stockinette stitches makes this a fun project for the novice knitter. Blanket stitch embroidery around the edges adds a touch of whimsy. Designed by Bonnie Franz.**

### SIZES
Instructions are written for size 2. Changes for 4 and 6 are in parentheses.

### KNITTED MEASUREMENTS
- Chest 27 (29, 31)"/68.5 (73.5, 78.5)cm
- Length 14 (15¼, 16½)"/35.5 (39, 42)cm
- Upper arm 12½ (13¼, 14½)"/32 (33.5, 37)cm

### MATERIALS
- 2 (3, 4) 1¾oz/50g skeins (each approx 118yd/108m) of Rowan *Summer Tweed* (silk/cotton ⑤) in #511 blue (MC)
- 2 skeins in #510 purple (A)
- 1 skein in #501 lilac (B)
- One pair size 8 (5mm) needles *or size to obtain gauge*
- Stitch markers

### GAUGES
- 16 sts and 26 rows to 4"/10cm over garter st using size 8 (5mm) needles.
- 16 sts and 20 rows to 4"/10cm over St st using size 8 (5mm) needles.
*Take time to check gauges.*

### BACK
With MC, cast on 54 (58, 62) sts. Work in garter st until piece measures 14 (15¼, 16½)"/35.5 (39, 42)cm. Bind off all sts.

### FRONT
Work as for back until piece measures 12 (12½, 13¾)"/30.5 (32, 35)cm from beg.
**Neck shaping**
**Next row (RS)** Work 22 (24, 25) sts, join a 2nd ball of yarn and bind off center 10 (10, 12) sts, work to end. Working both sides at once, dec 1 st from each neck edge every other row 6 (6, 5) times. Work even until piece measures same length as back. Bind off rem 16 (18, 20) sts each side for shoulders.

### SLEEVES
With A, cast on 30 (31, 32) sts. Work in k1, p1 rib for 1 row. Beg with a WS row, work in St st, AT SAME TIME, inc 1 st each side every 4th row 7 (6, 9) times, every 6th row 3 (5, 4) times—50 (53, 58) sts. Work even until piece measures 10½ (12, 13)"/26.5 (30.5, 33)cm from beg. Bind off.

### POCKETS
(make 2)
With A, cast on 20 sts. Work in St st until piece measures 3½"/9cm. Bind off.

## FINISHING

Sew shoulder seams. Place markers 6¼ (6½, 7¼)"/16 (16.5, 18.5)cm down from each shoulder edge. Sew in sleeves between markers. Sew side and sleeve seams.

Sew pockets to front (see photo for placement). Using B, embroider buttonhole stitch edging around lower edge of body sleeves, around neck and pockets.

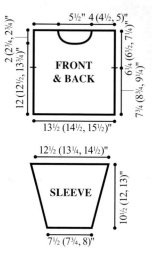

# CHENILLE SCARF

*Natural wonder*

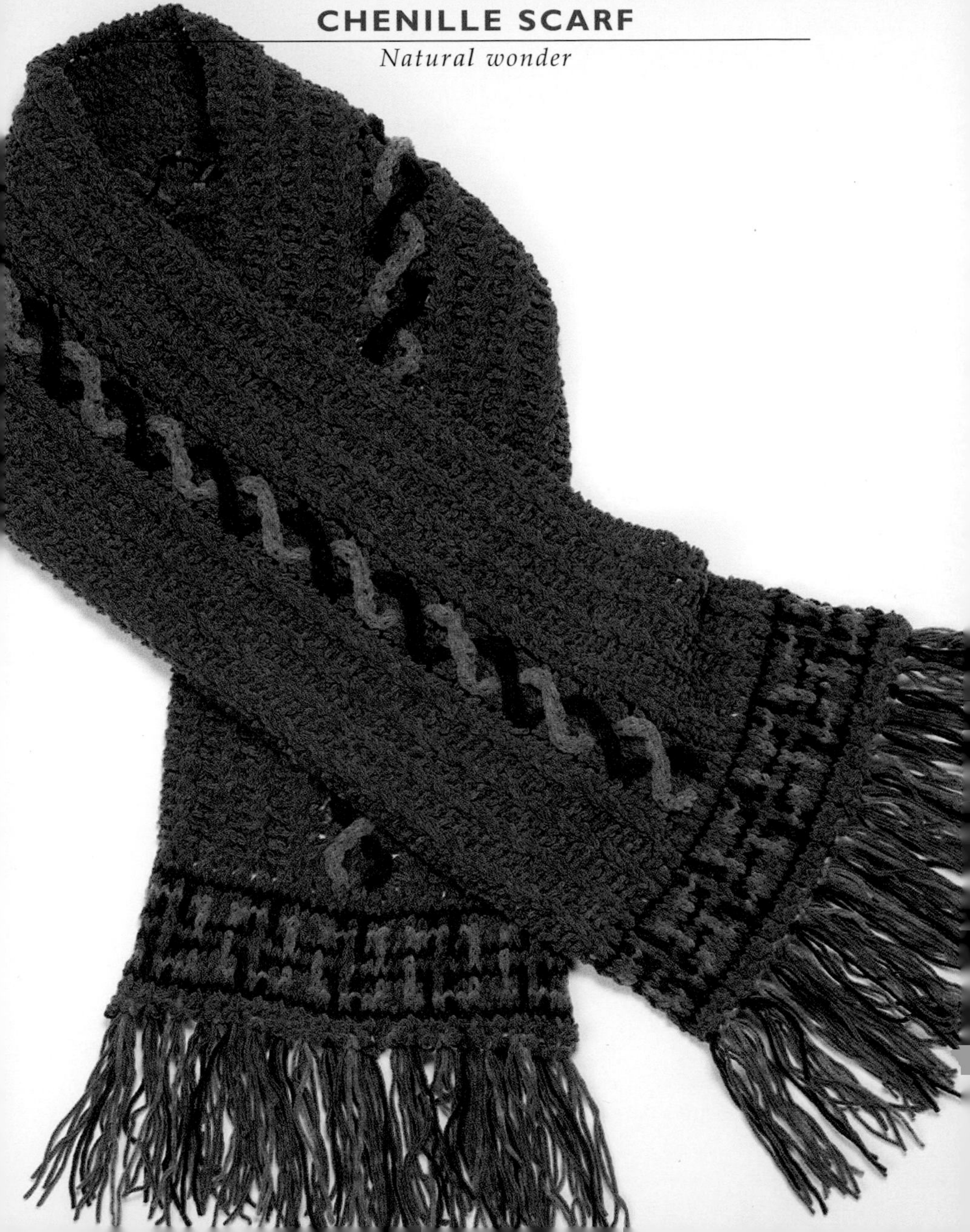

**This chenille yarn feels so soft and cozy around the neck, and the woodland pallette adds to the warmth. Three-colored cables are easy to knit with a little practice. Designed by Betsy Westman.**

## KNITTED MEASUREMENTS
- 9" x 56"/23 x 142cm (without fringe)

## MATERIALS
- 4 1¾oz/50g skeins (each approx 140yd/128m) of K1C2, LLC *Velvety Chenille* (wool/nylon ④) in #523 green (A)
- One skein each in #575 brown (B) and #841 tan (C)
- One pair size 9 (5.5mm) needles *or size to obtain gauge*
- Cable needle
- Size H/8 (5mm) crochet hook

## GAUGE
20 sts and 24 rows to 4"/10cm over backround pat using size 9 (5.5mm) needles. *Take time to check gauge.*

## STITCH GLOSSARY
**Right Twist (RT)**
K2tog leaving sts on LH needle, insert RH needle between the 2 sts just worked and k the first st again, sl both sts from needle tog.
**Note**
When working two-color cables, always match the colors from the previous row.

**4-St RC**
Sl 2 sts to cn and hold to *back*, k2, k2 from cn.
**4-St LC**
Sl 2 sts to cn and hold to *front*, k2, k2 from cn.
**5-St RC**
Sl 3 sts to cn and hold to *back*, k2, sl center st from cn back to LH needle and k it, k2 from cn.

## SCARF
With A, cast on 46 sts.
**Row 1 (RS)** *K2tog, yo; rep from * to last 2 sts, k2tog—45 sts.
**Row 2** *K1, p1; rep from * to end.
**Beg chart 1**
Work in St st, beg with row 1 and work 9-st color rep 5 times. Cont as established through chart row 11. Change to A.
**Next row (WS)** Purl.
**Next row (RS)** *K2tog, yo; rep from * end k1. P 1 row.
**Beg chart 2**
Work rows 1-16 of chart in colors as indicated, rep rows 1-16 until piece measures 53"/134.5cm from beg, end with a RS row. Change to A.
**Next row (WS)** Purl.
**Next row (RS)** K1, yo, *k2tog, yo; rep from * end k1. P 1 row.
**Beg chart 1**
Work in St st, beg with row 1 and work 9-st color rep 5 times. Cont as established through chart row 11. Change to A.
**Next row (WS)** Purl

**Next row (RS)** *K1, p1; rep from * to end.

**Next row (WS)** *P2tog, yo; rep from *, end p1—46 sts. Bind off.

**FINISHING**

**Fringe**

With A, B and C, cut 5"/12.5cm lengths. Using the holes made on edges of scarf, tie fringe using 3 strands; 2 of A and 1 of either B or C, alternating each fringe.

**CHART 1**

9 sts

11
9
7
5
3
1

**Color Key**

■ Green (A)
■ Brown (B)
□ Tan (C)

**Stitch Key**

Note: Work all sts matching colors as shown

□ K on RS, p on WS          ⊠ RT

⊟ P on RS, k on WS          4-st RC

⊙ Yo                        4-st LC

⊠ K2tog                     5-st RC

⊠ SSK

**CHART 2**

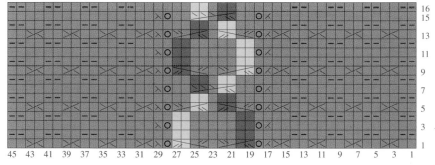

16
15
13
11
9
7
5
3
1

45  43  41  39  37  35  33  31  29  27  25  23  21  19  17  15  13  11  9  7  5  3  1

# TUBE SOCKS
*Show your stripes*

**Lila Chin's super striped tube socks have a ribbed body for elasticity and stockinette stitch toes for a more comfortable fit. The absence of a heel means they can be knit in no time.**

## MATERIALS

- 2 1¾oz/50g skeins (each approx 175yd/158m) of Koigu Wool Designs *Koigu Premium Merino* (wool ③) in #2326 dk blue (A)
- 1 skein in #2323 lt blue (B)
- One set (4) size 4 (3.5mm) dpn *or size to obtain gauge*

## GAUGE

28 sts and 34 rows to 4"/10cm over k2, p2 rib (unstretched) using size 4 (3.5mm) needles.

*Take time to check gauge.*

## STRIPE PAT

Working in k2, p2 rib, work *6 rnds A, 4 rnds B; rep from * (10 rnds) for stripe pat.

## SOCKS

With A, cast on 52 sts. Divide sts over 3 needles as foll: 13 sts on needle 1, 26 sts on needle 2, 13 sts on needle 3. Join, being careful not to twist sts. Pm at beg of rnd and sl every rnd. Work in stripe pat until piece measures 16"/40.5cm, or desired length, end with 4 rows B. Change to St st and A.

**Shape toe**

**Dec rnd** *Needle 1* K to last 2 sts, k2tog; *Needle 2* SKP, k to last 2 sts, k2tog; *Needle 3* SKP, k to end. Work 1 rnd even. Rep last 2 rnds until 20 sts rem. Close toe with kitchener st.

# RIBBED CAP

*Hat's off!*

**Styled for both men and women, this hat can be knit in just a few hours. Stripe it in your favorite team's colors, or make it solid. Designed by Veronica Manno.**

## KNITTED MEASUREMENTS

■ Circumference 18½"/47cm (due to elasticity of the rib, this hat will fit most sizes)

## MATERIALS

■ 2 1¾oz/50g skeins (each approx 148yd/133m) of Dale of Norway *Sisik* (wool ④) in # purple (MC)

■ 1 skeins in #163 lt green (CC)

■ One pair size 9 (5.5mm) needles *or size to obtain gauge*

## GAUGE

15 sts and 20 rows to 4"/10cm over k3, p2 rib (slightly stretched) using size 9 (5.5mm) needles and 2 strands of yarn held tog.
*Take time to check gauge.*

## NOTE

Work with 2 strands of yarn held tog throughout.

## K3, P2 RIB

(multiple of 5 sts)
**Row 1 (RS)** *K3, p2; rep from * to end.
**Row 2** K the knit sts and p the purl sts.
Rep row 2 for k3, p2 rib.

## STRIPE PATTERN

*Work 8 rows MC, 4 rows CC; rep from * once more.

## HAT

With 2 strands of MC held tog, cast on 70 sts. Work in k3, p2 rib and stripe pat for 24 rows. Piece measures approx 5"/12.5cm.
**Shape top**
**Next row (RS)** [K2tog, k1, p2, k3, p2] 7 times—63 sts. Work 3 rows even.
**Next row** [K2, p2, k2tog, k1, p2] 7 times—56 sts. Work 3 rows even.
**Next row** [K2, p2tog, k2, p2] 7 times—49 sts. Work 1 row even.
**Next row** [K2, p1, k2, p2tog] 7 times—42 sts. Work 1 row even.
**Next row** [K2tog, p1, k2, p1] 7 times—35 sts. Work 1 row even.
**Next row** [K1, p1, k2tog, p1] 7 times—28 sts.
**Next row** [P2tog, p2] 7 times—21 sts.
**Next row** [K1, k2tog] 7 times—14 sts.
**Next row** [P2tog] 7 times—7 sts.
**Next row** [K2tog] twice, k3tog—3 sts.
Cut yarn and draw through rem sts.

## FINISHING

Block very lightly. With MC and CC, make 3"/7.5cm pom pom. Sew back seam. Sew pom pom to top of hat.

# MOHAIR CARDIGAN
*Buttons & Bows*

**Sewn-on grosgrain ribbon bows and delicate pearl buttons turn this basic cardigan into a delightful garment that will get oooh's from all the girls. Designed by Jean Guirguis.**

### SIZES

Instructions are written for Child's size 2. Changes for 3 and 4 are in parentheses.

### KNITTED MEASUREMENTS

■ Chest (buttoned) 27 (29, 31)"/68.5 (73.5, 78.5)cm

■ Length 12¾ (13½, 14)"/32.5 (34, 35.5)cm

■ Upper arm 11½ (13, 14)"/29 (33, 35.5)cm

### MATERIALS

■ 5 (6, 6) 1½oz/42g skeins (each approx 90yd/82m) of Classic Elite Yarns *LaGran Mohair* (wool ④) in #6527 red

■ One pair size 8 (5mm) needles *or size to obtain gauge*

■ Stitch holders

■ 4 yds ¼"/6mm black grosgrain ribbon

■ Seven ¼"/6mm buttons

■ Black sewing thread and needle

### GAUGE

15 sts and 20 rows to 4"/10cm over St st using size 8 (5mm) needles.
*Take time to check gauge.*

### BACK

Cast on 50 (54, 58) sts. Work in garter st for 1"/2.5cm. Change to St st and work until piece measures 12¾ (13½, 14)"/32.5 (34, 35.5)cm from beg. Bind off all sts.

### LEFT FRONT

Cast on 27 (29, 31) sts. Work in garter st for 1"/2.5cm, end with a WS row.

**Next row (RS)** Work in St st to last 4 sts, work in garter st to end (for buttonband). Cont in pat as established until piece measures 10¾ (11½, 12)"/27 (29, 30.5)cm from beg, end with a RS row.

**Neck shaping**

**Next row (WS)** Work 4 sts and sl to a holder, bind off 3 sts (neck edge), work to end. Cont to bind off from neck edge 3 sts once more, 2 sts 3 times. Work even until same length as back. Bind off rem 11 (13, 15) sts for shoulder. Place markers on band for 6 buttons, the first one in center of garter st band at lower edge, the last one 1"/2.5cm below neck shaping, and 4 others spaced evenly between.

### RIGHT FRONT

Work as for left front, reversing all shaping and placement of buttonband, and work buttonholes opposite markers on RS rows as foll: Work 2 sts, k2tog, yo, work to end.

## SLEEVES

Cast on 24 (26, 28) sts. Work in garter st for 1"/2.5cm. Change to St st, inc 1 st each side every 2nd row 4 (6, 8) times, every 4th row 6 (5, 4) times—44 (48, 52) sts. Work even until piece measures 8½"/21.5cm from beg. Bind off.

## FINISHING

Block pieces to measurements. Sew shoulder seams.

### Collar

With RS facing, pick up and k62 sts evenly around neck edge, including sts from holders. Work in garter st for ½"/1.5cm. Work another buttonhole on right front band as before. Work even until collar measures 1"/2.5cm. Bind off.

Place markers 5¾ (6½, 7)"/14.5 (16.5, 18)cm down from each shoulder edge. Sew in sleeves between markers. Sew side and sleeve seams. Sew on buttons. Make 25 small bows and sew on cardigan.

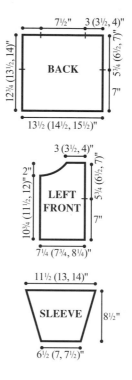

7½"    3 (3½, 4)"

12¾ (13½, 14)"    BACK    5¾ (6½, 7)"    7"

13½ (14½, 15½)"

3 (3½, 4)"

10¾ (11½, 12)"    2"    LEFT FRONT    5¾ (6½, 7)"    7"

7¼ (7¾, 8¼)"

11½ (13, 14)"

SLEEVE    8½"

6½ (7, 7½)"

**You become the artist when Trendsetter Yarns Gel is applied to the finished top to create a tie-dye-look pattern. The tiny crocheted straps and delicate ruffled edges are a sure bet for the hip teen. Designed by Fayla Reiss.**

## SIZES

Instructions are written for Girl's size 10. Changes for 12, 14 and 16 are in parentheses.

## KNITTED MEASUREMENTS

- Chest 27 (29, 31, 33)"/68.5 (73.5, 78.5, 84)cm
- Length 12 (12¼, 12½, 13)"/30.5 (31, 32, 33)cm

## MATERIALS

- .70 oz/20g balls (each approx 95yd/85m) of Trendsetter Yarns *Sunshine* (rayon/nylon ④) in #53 teal
- One pair size 6 (4mm) needles *or size to obtain gauge*
- Size F/5 (4mm) crochet hook
- Trendsetter Yarns Gel (Note that this gel product only works on rayon, cotton, or blends of these two. It does not work on wool, polyester or acrylic.)

## GAUGE

21 sts and 30 rows to 4"/10cm over St st using size 6 (4mm) needles.
*Take time to check gauge.*

## BACK

Cast on 72 (76, 82, 86) sts. Work in St st for 9"/23cm.

**Armhole shaping**

Bind off 3 sts at beg of next 2 rows.
**Next row (RS)** K2, k2tog, work to last 4 sts, ssk, k2. Work 1 row even. Rep last 2 rows 7 (8, 9, 10) times more—50 (52, 56, 58) sts. Work even until armhole measures 3 (3¼, 3½, 4)"/7.5 (8, 9, 10)cm. Bind off.

## FRONT

Work as for back.

## STRAPS

(make 4)
With crochet hook, chain approx 8"/20.5cm long. Sl st in 2nd ch from hook and in each ch to end. Make a knot in each, approx 2"/5cm from one end. Sew 2 straps to front and back of each side, with 1 knot facing front and 1 knot facing back.

## CROCHETED EDGINGS

With RS facing and crochet hook, work along lower edge of back as foll: Work 3 sc in each cast-on st. Fasten off. Work in same way along lower edge of front and along front and back necks.

## FINISHING

Lay pieces flat and apply gel in pattern as in photo (or as desired). When the color is as desired, place pieces in cold water with

a sprinkle of powder (supplied with gel).
Rinse until all color stops bleeding. Let
dry. See photos below.
Sew side seams.

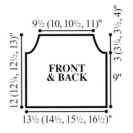

9½ (10, 10½, 11)"

12 (12¼, 12½, 13)"

3 (3¼, 3½, 4)"

FRONT
& BACK

9"

13½ (14½, 15½, 16½)"

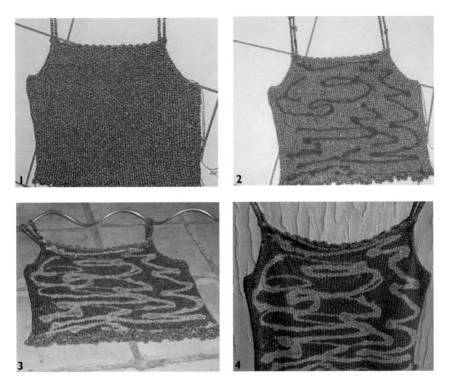

1 Lay pieces on a flat surface. 2 Apply gel to knitted fabric in desired design.
3 Place pieces in cold water with a sprinkle of powder and continue rinsing until the
colors stop bleeding. 4 After pieces have dried, sew the seams.

# SEED STITCH MITTENS
*Loving hands*

*For Beginner Knitters*

**Both mittens are worked identically, making this the perfect project for a new knitter. Roomy in size, they fit the average adult; simply adjust the length of the hand and thumb for a custom fit. Designed by Veronica Manno.**

## MATERIALS

- 3 1¾oz/50g balls (each approx 60yd/54m) of Lion Brand Yarn Company *Kool Wool* (acrylic/wool ⑤) in #113 red
- One pair size 9 (5.5mm) needles *or size to obtain gauge*
- Stitch holders

## GAUGE

12 sts and 24 rows to 4"/10cm over seed st using size 9 (5.5mm) needles.
*Take time to check gauge.*

## SEED STITCH

**Row 1 (RS)** *K1, p1; rep from * to end.
**Row 2** K the purl sts and p the knit sts.
Rep row 2 for seed st.

## LEFT MITTEN

Cast on 30 sts. Work in k2, p2 rib for 2"/5cm. Work in seed st for 1½"/4cm. Cut yarn.

**Beg thumb**
Sl 12 sts to a holder, join a 2nd ball of yarn and work 6 sts, sl rem 12 sts to a holder.

**Next row** Inc 1 st in first st, work 2 sts, inc 1 st in next st, work 1 st, inc 1 st in last st—9 sts. Cont in seed st for 12 rows.
**Next (dec) row** [K1, k2tog] 3 times—6 sts.
**Next (dec) row** [K2tog] 3 times. Cut yarn and draw through rem 3 sts. Fasten off.

**Hand**
Rejoin yarn to sts from first holder, work 12 sts in seed st, pick up 3 sts each side of thumb, work 12 sts from 2nd holder—30 sts. Work even until piece measures 9"/23cm from beg, end with a WS row.

**Top shaping**
**Row 1 (RS)** K1, k2tog, k10, [k2tog] twice, k10, k2tog, k1—26 sts.
**Rows 2, 4 and 6** Work even in seed st.
**Row 3** K1, k2tog, k8, [k2tog] twice, k8, k2tog, k1—22 sts.
**Row 5** K1, k2tog, k6, [k2tog] twice, k6, k2tog, k1—18 sts.
**Row 7** [K2tog] 9 times. Cut yarn and draw through rem 9 sts. Fasten off.

## RIGHT MITTEN

Work as for left mitten (mittens are reversible).

## FINISHING

Sew side seams.

# CAP AND BOOTIES

*Simply irresistible*

*For Intermediate Knitters*

**Delightful cap and booties are designed by Mari Lynn Patrick and knit in simple pattern combinations reminiscent of fishermen's knits. Cap is knit flat and then seamed along the crown sides; the booties are also knit flat beginning at the sole edge.**

## SIZES

Cap and booties fit infant newborn to 6 months old.

## KNITTED MEASUREMENTS

*Cap*
■ Crown circumference 17"/43cm

*Booties*
■ Length of sole 4¼"/11cm

*Leg*
■ 2"/5cm

## MATERIALS

■ 2 1¾oz/50g balls (each approx 138yd/125m) of Debbie Bliss Yarns/KFI *Baby Cashmerino* (wool/microfibre/cashmere ②) in #303 lt grey
■ One pair size 3 (3.25mm) needles or size to obtain gauge
■ Cable needle

## GAUGES

■ 26 sts and 36 rows to 4"/10cm over basketweave and ladder st pats using size 3 (3.25mm) needles
■ One 6-stitch cable panel = ¾"/2cm wide.
*Take time to check gauges.*

## BASKETWEAVE STITCH

(multiple of 4 sts plus 2)
**Row 1 (RS)** K2, *p2, k2; rep from * to end.
**Row 2** P2, *k2, p2; rep from * to end.
**Row 3** Rep row 2.
**Row 4** Rep row 1. Rep rows 1-4 for basketweave st.

## 6-STITCH CABLE

**Row 1 (RS)** P1, k4, p1.
**Row 2** K1, p4, k1.
**Row 3** P1, sl 2 sts to cn and hold to *back*, k2, k2 from cn, p1.
**Row 4** Rep row 2.
Rep rows 1-4 for 6-stitch cable.

## LADDER STITCH

(any number of sts)
**Row 1 (RS)** Knit.
**Rows 2, 3 and 4** Purl.
Rep rows 1-4 for ladder st.

## CAP

Beg at lower edge, cast on 111 sts. Work in garter st for 10 rows.
**Next row (RS)** Bind off 9 sts (the last st from the bind-off is the selvage st), work 10 sts in basketweave st, p1, 8 sts in ladder st, 6-st cable panel, 10 sts in basketweave st, 6-st cable panel, 9 sts in ladder st, 6-st cable panel, 10 sts in basketweave st, 6-st cable panel, 8 sts in ladder st, p1, 10 sts in basketweave st, k1 (selvage st), then with a separate short length of yarn, bind off rem 9 sts—93 sts.

Cont in pats as established until piece measures 3½"/9cm from beg.

**Shape Top**

Bind off 9 sts at beg of next 8 rows—21 sts. Cont as established on center 21 sts for 8¼"/21cm or until piece fits along side bound-off edges and down the side to the lower garter band. Bind off.

**FINISHING**

Block lightly to measurements. Foll diagram, sew lower garter band tog matching A to A (this is center back seam). Sew straight B sections to angled C sections. Sew half of each D section along final 21-st bind-off to first and last 9 sts bound-off along lower edge. Sew crown section to bound off side edges and across lower garter band.

**BOOTIES**

Beg at sole edge, cast on 56 sts.

**Row 1 (RS)** Work 10 sts in basketweave st, p1, 14 sts in ladder st, 6-st cable panel, 14 sts in ladder st, p1, 10 sts in basketweave st. Work even in pats as estab-

lished for 6 rows.
**Dec row 1 (RS)** Work to 2 sts before 6-st cable, p2tog, work 6-st cable, p2tog tbl, work to end.
**Dec row 2 (WS)** Work to 2 sts before 6-st cable, p2tog tbl, work 6-st cable, p2tog, work to end. **Dec row 3** Work to 2 sts before 6-st cable, k2tog, work 6-st cable, SKP, work to end.
**Dec row 4** Rep dec row 2. Rep last 4 rows once more.
**Next row** Rep dec row 1.
**Next row** Rep dec row 2.

**Next row** Rep dec row 3—34 sts. Work even for 1"/2.5cm. Then work 6 rows even in garter st. Bind off.

**FINISHING**
Block pieces lightly. Fold in half along cast-on edges and seam cast-on edge for sole seam. Sew back edge of leg to finish bootie.

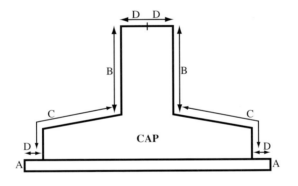

## Very Easy Very Vogue

**A simple striking cable graces the front of this elegant shell. Luxurious silk tape yarn provides plenty of elasticity, sheen, and softness. Designed by Veronica Manno.**

### SIZES

Instructions are written for size Small. Changes for Medium and Large are in parentheses.

### KNITTED MEASUREMENTS

- Bust 33 (36, 39)"/84 (91.5, 99)cm
- Length 19½ (20, 20½)"/49.5 (51, 52)cm

### MATERIALS

- 2 (2, 3) 1¾oz/50g balls (each approx 164yd/148m) of Classic Elite Yarns *Playful Weekend* (silk ⑥) in #20328 blue
- One pair each sizes 11 and 15 (8 and 10mm) needles *or size to obtain gauge*
- Cable needle

### GAUGE

12 sts and 14 rows to 4"/10cm over St st using large needles.
*Take time to check gauge.*

### STITCH GLOSSARY

**4-st RC** Sl 2 sts to cn and hold to *back*, k2, k2 from cn.

**4-st LC** Sl 2 sts to cn and hold to *front*, k2, k2 from cn.

### CABLE PANEL

(over 12 sts)
**Rows I and 3 (RS)** P2, k8, p2.
**Row 2 and all WS rows** K the knit sts and p the purl sts.
**Row 5** P2, 4-st LC, 4-st RC, p2.
**Row 6** Rep row 2
Rep rows 1-6 for cable panel.

### BACK

With smaller needles, cast on 50 (54, 58) sts. Work in k2, p2 rib for 1½"/4cm. Change to larger needles and work in St st until piece measures 11"/28cm from beg.
**Armhole shaping**
Bind off 2 sts at beg of next 2 rows.
**Next (dec) row (RS)** K1, k2tog, work to last 3 sts, ssk, k1. Work 1 row even. Rep last 2 rows 3 (4, 4) times more—38 (40, 44) sts. Work even until armhole measures 7 (7½, 8)"/18 (19, 20.5)cm.
**Neck shaping**
Work 16 (17, 19) sts, join a 2nd ball of yarn and bind off center 6 sts, work to end. Working both sides at once, dec 1 st at each neck edge *every* row 5 times. Bind off rem 11 (12, 14) sts each side for shoulders.

### FRONT

With smaller needles, cast on 50 (54, 58) sts. Work in k2, p2 rib for 1½"/4cm. Change to larger needles.
**Next row (RS)** Work 19 (21, 23) sts in St st, work row 1 of cable panel over 12 sts, work in St st to end. Cont in pats as estab-

lished, work as for back until armhole
measures 5½ (6, 6½)"/14 (15, 16.5)cm

**Neck shaping**
Work 16 (17, 19) sts, join a 2nd ball of
yarn and bind off center 6 sts, work to end.
Working both sides at once, dec 1 at at
each neck edge every other row 5 times.
Work even until piece measures same as
back to shoulders. Bind off rem 11 (12,
14) sts each side for shoulders.

**FINISHING**
Sew shoulder and side seams.

# KID'S SLIP STITCH PULLOVER

*To dye for!*

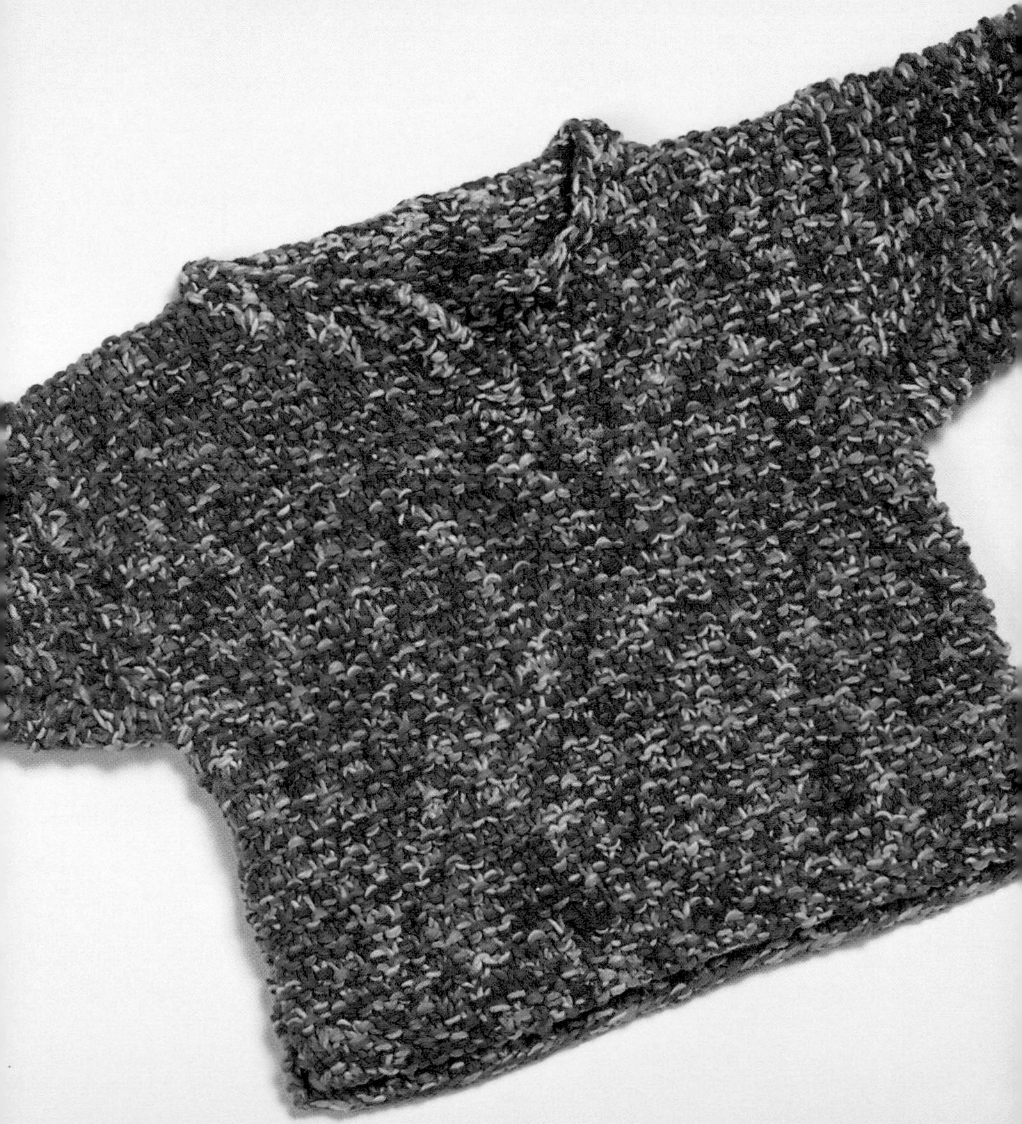

## For Beginner Knitters

This cute kid's top knits up quickly with two strands of yarn held together using a simple slip stitch. The variegated coloring of the yarn adds panache! Designed by Joanne Yordanou.

### SIZES

Instructions are written for size Child's 2. Changes for 4 and 6 are in parentheses.

### KNITTED MEASUREMENTS

- Chest 27½ (30½, 32½)"/70 (77.5, 82.5)cm
- Length 13½ (14½, 16)"/34 (37, 40.5)cm
- Upper arm 11¾ (13¼, 14¼)"/30 (33.5, 36)cm

### MATERIALS

- 7 (7, 8) 1¾oz/50g skeins (each approx 116yd/104m) of Naturally/S.R. Kerzer, Ltd. *Cotton Fizz* (cotton/wool ③) in #602 turquoise
- One pair size 10 (6mm) needles *or size to obtain gauge*
- Size 10 (6mm) circular needle, 24"/60cm long

### GAUGE

16 sts and 24 rows to 4"/10cm over St st using size 10 (6mm) needles using 2 strands of yarn held tog.
*Take time to check gauge.*

### SLIP STITCH PATTERN

**Rows 1 (RS) and 2** Knit.
**Row 3** K1, *sl 1, k1; rep from * to end.
**Row 4** K1, *bring yarn to front (yf), sl 1, bring yarn to back (yb), k1; rep from * to end.
**Rows 5 and 6** Knit.
**Row 7** K2, *sl 1, k1; rep from * to last st, k1.
**Row 8** K2, *yf, sl 1, yb, k1; rep from * to last st, k1.
Rep these 8 rows for sl st pat.

### SEED STITCH

**Row 1 (RS)** *K1, p1; rep from * to end.
**Row 2** K the purl sts and p the knit sts.
Rep row 2 for seed st.

### BACK

With 2 strands of yarn held tog, cast on 49 (55, 59) sts. Work in seed st for 4 rows. **Next row (RS)** Knit, inc 6 sts evenly across—55 (61, 65) sts. Beg with row 2, work in sl st pat until piece measures 13 (14, 15½)"/33 (35.5, 39.5)cm from beg, end with a WS row.

**Shoulder shaping**
Bind off 8 (9, 9) sts at beg of next 2 rows, 7 (9, 10) sts at beg of next 2 rows. Bind off rem 25 (25, 27) sts for back neck.

### FRONT

Work as for back until piece measures 9 (9½, 11)"/23 (24, 28)cm from beg, end with a WS row.

**Placket shaping**
**Next row (RS)** Work 26 (29, 31) sts, join a 2nd ball of yarn and bind off center 3 sts, work to end. Working both sides at once, work even in sl st pat until placket measures 2 (2½, 2½)"/5 (6.5, 6.5)cm, end with a WS row.

**Neck shaping**
Bind off 3 sts from each neck once, dec 1 st *every* row 8 (8, 9) times—15 (18, 19) sts. Work even until piece measures same as back to shoulders. Shape shoulders as for back.

SLEEVES
With 2 strands of yarn held tog, cast on 28 (30, 32) sts. Work in seed st for 4 rows.
**Next row (RS)** Knit, inc 5 sts evenly across—33 (35, 37) sts. Beg with row 2, work in sl st pat, AT SAME TIME, inc 1 st each side, working inc sts in pat, every 2nd (2nd, 6th) row 4 (1, 5) times, every

4th row 3 (8, 5) times —47 (53, 57) sts. Work even until piece measures 5½ (7½, 9)"/14 (19, 23)cm from beg. Bind off.

FINISHING
Do not block. Sew shoulder seams.
**Front placket**
(make 2)
With 2 strands of yarn held tog, cast on 3 sts. Work in seed st until placket measures 2 (2½, 2½)"/5 (6.5, 6.5)cm. Bind off. Sew plackets into opening placing right front placket over left front.

With circular needle, beg at placket, pick up and k18 sts along right front neck, 25 (25, 27) sts across back neck, and 18 sts along left front neck—61 (61, 63) sts. Work in seed st for 3 rows. Bind off.

Place markers 5¾ (6½, 7)"/14.5 (16.5, 18)cm down from each shoulder edge. Sew in sleeves between markers. Sew side and sleeve seams.

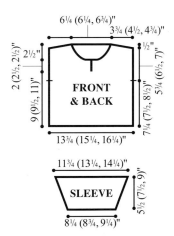

6¼ (6¼, 6¾)"

3¾ (4½, 4¾)"

2 (2½, 2½)"    2½"    ½"

9 (9½, 11)"

FRONT & BACK

7¼ (7½, 8½)"    5¾ (6½, 7)"

13¾ (15¼, 16¼)"

11¾ (13¼, 14¼)"

SLEEVE

5½ (7½, 9)"

8¼ (8¾, 9¼)"

**Garter stitch stripes make the perfect fabric for a knitted purse. Sturdy and colorful, you can use it as an everyday tote or a cool knitting bag. Designed by Charlotte Parry.**

## KNITTED MEASUREMENTS
- 10" x 11"/25.5 x 28cm

## MATERIALS
- 1 4oz/113g skein (each approx 125yd/114m) of Brown Sheep Yarn Co. *Lambs Pride Bulky* (wool ⑤) each in #M-100 purple (A), #M-180 red (B), #M-14 gold (C), #M-38 pink (D), #M-57 blue (E) and #M-110 orange (F)
- One pair size 10½ (6.5mm) needles *or size to obtain gauge*
- Size 10½ (6.5mm) circular needle, 24"/60cm long
- Stitch markers
- Purse handles #23900 by M&J Trimming

## GAUGE
14 sts and 28 rows to 4"/10cm over garter st using size 10½ (6.5mm) needles.
*Take time to check gauge.*

## STRIPE PATTERN
Work in garter st and stripe pat as foll: *2 rows A, 2 rows B, 2 rows C, 2 rows D, 2 rows E, 2 rows F; rep from * (12 rows) for stripe pat.

## NOTE
When working garter st in the rnd, work k 1 rnd, p 1 rnd.

## BOTTOM
With A, cast on 38 sts. Work in garter st and stripe pat until piece measures 3½"/9cm. Bind off.

## SIDES
With RS facing and A, beg at corner and pick up and k12 sts along one short edge, 38 sts along one long edge, 12 sts along other short edge, 38 sts along other long edge—100 sts. Join, being careful not to twist sts. Pm at end of rnd and slip every rnd. Work in garter st and stripe pat until piece measures 10"/25.5cm from beg. Bind off.

## FINISHING
Block pieces. Sew on handles to inside of front and back. Cut a piece of sturdy cardboard 3½" x 11"/9 x 28cm for bottom of bag.

# MOHAIR SCARF

*Wrap around*

*For Beginner Knitters*

**Chi Ling Moy chose soft shades of luxurious mohair to fashion this captivating scarf. While the drop stitch pattern may be a little tricky for beginners, the technique can easily be mastered. Added bonus: it looks great on both sides!**

KNITTED MEASUREMENTS
- Approx 7½" x 56"/19cm x 142cm

MATERIALS
- 1 skein (each approx 225yd/202m) of Mountain Colors *Mohair* (mohair ⑥) in sagebrush
- One pair size 9 (5.5mm) needles *or size to obtain gauge*

GAUGE
12 sts and 14 rows to 4"/10cm over drop st pat using size 9 (5.5mm) needles.
*Take time to check gauge.*

DROP STITCH PATTERN
**Row 1 (RS)** *K1, wrapping yarn 3 times around needle; rep from * to end.
**Row 2** Knit, dropping extra wrapped sts.
**Rows 3 and 4** Knit.
Rep rows 1-4 for drop st pat.

SCARF
Cast on 22 sts. K 3 rows. Work in drop st pat until piece measures 55½"/141cm from beg, or until there are a few yards left (enough for 3 more rows). K 3 rows. Bind off.

*For Beginner Knitters*

**This cable-knit belt is trimmed with lengths of beaded fringe ties for a hip sense of style. Mari Lynn Patrick designed this belt in a substantial ribbed cable with garter trim.**

**KNITTED MEASUREMENTS**

Approx 3" x 33"/7.5cm x 84cm, slightly stretched without fringe

**MATERIALS**

- 2 2½oz/71g balls (each approx 120yd/109m) of Lily *Sugar 'N Cream* (cotton ④) in #00082 tan
- One pair size 6 (4mm) needles *or size to obtain gauge*
- Assorted bone, wood and gold beads available through *Beadazzled*, 501 N. Charles St., Baltimore, MD 21201, Telephone: (410) 837-2323

**GAUGE**

20 sts to 3"/6.5cm and 24 rows to 4"/10cm over cabled pat using size 6 (4mm) needles. *Take time to check gauge.*

**NOTE**

To make a belt without fringe in a hip-slung style, use hidden large hook and eye closures to fasten belt closed.

**BELT**

Cast on 20 sts. **Row 1 (WS)** Knit.
**Row 2 (RS)** P1, k1, k2, [p1, k1] 3 times, [k1, p1] 3 times, k2, k1, p1.
**Row 3** K1, p1, k2, [k1, p1] 3 times, [p1, k1] 3 times, k2, p1, k1. Rep rows 2 and 3 three times more.
**Row 10 (RS)** P1, k1, k2, p1, sl next 5 sts to cn and hold to *back*, k1, p1, k1, p1, k1, then k1, p1, k1, p1, k1 from cn, p1, k2, k1, p1. Work even for 9 rows. Rep last 10 rows for cable pat 18 times more. Work even for 8 rows. K 1 row on WS. Bind off knitwise.

**FRINGE**

Cut 30 44"/112cm lengths for each fringe. Working from WS of belt, fold each length in half and place 15 single fringes at each end of belt. Slide beads in a varied pattern to ends of fringe. Knot to stay in place.

# TODDLER VEST
*Tweedy pie*

**Jil Eaton designed this chic vest for tiny tots. Two strands of different colored yarns creates the tweedy effect; add contrasting whimsical buttons to complete the look.**

## SIZES

Instructions are written for size 1 year. Changes for 2 and 3 years are in parentheses.

## KNITTED MEASUREMENTS

▓ Chest (buttoned) 22½ (24½, 27)"/57 (62, 68.5)cm

▓ Length 9½ (10, 10½)"/24 (25.5, 26.5)cm

## MATERIALS

▓ 1 1¾oz/50g skeins (each approx 138yd/124m) of Manos Del Uruguay/Design Source (wool ⑤) each in #11 navy (A) and #2330 pistachio (B)

▓ One pair size 13 (9mm) needles *or size to obtain gauge*

▓ Size F/5 (4mm) crochet hook

▓ Stitch holders

▓ Four ½"/13mm buttons

## GAUGE

11 sts and 15 rows to 4"/10cm over St st with 1 strand each A and B held tog using size 13 (9mm) needles.
*Take time to check gauge.*

## NOTES

**1** Body is worked in one piece to armhole, then both fronts and back are worked separately to shoulder.

**2** Use 1 strand each A and B held tog throughout.

## BODY

With one strand each A and B held together, cast on 61 (67, 73) sts. Work in k1, p1 rib as foll: **Next row (RS)** P1, *k1, p1; rep from * to end.

**Next row** K1, *p1, k1; rep from * to end.

**Next row** P1, k1, p1, work in St st to last 3 sts, inc 1 st in center of row, end p1, k1, p1—62 (68, 74) sts. Cont in St st, working first and last 3 sts in rib, until piece measures 5½"/14cm from beg, end with a WS row.

### Divide for fronts and back

Work 11 (12, 13) sts and place on holder for right front, bind off 8 (9, 10) sts, work 24 (26, 28) sts for back, place rem 19 (21, 23) sts on holder for left front.

## BACK

Working on back sts only, cont in St st, working first and last 2 sts in garter st, until armhole measures 4 (4½, 5)"/10 (11.5, 12.5)cm. Place 5 (6, 7) sts on holder for right shoulder, bind off 14 sts, place rem 5 (6, 7) sts on holder for left shoulder.

## LEFT FRONT

With RS facing, rejoin 1 strand each A and B to work left front, bind off 8 (9, 10) sts for armhole, work in garter st for 2 sts, work in St st to last 3 sts, p1, k1 p1. Cont in St st, working 2 armhole sts in garter st and 3 side sts in rib until armhole measures 3 (3½, 4)"/7½ (9, 10)cm.

**Neck shaping**

**Next row (WS)** Rib 3 sts and place on a holder, bind off 2 sts, work to end.

**Next row** Work to last 2 sts, k2tog. Work even until same length as back. Place rem 5 (6, 7) sts on holder for shoulder.

### RIGHT FRONT

With RS facing, rejoin 1 strand each A and B to work right front, and work to correspond to left front, reversing neck shaping.

### FINISHING

Block piece to measurements. With wrong sides of fabric tog (this will create a ridge on the RS) and using 3-needle bind off, k shoulders tog.

**Neckband**

With RS facing and one strand each A and B held tog, work 3 sts from right front neck holder, pick up and k 27 sts evenly around neck edge, work 3 sts from left front neck holder—33 sts. Work in k1, p1 rib for 2 rows. Bind off.

With crochet hook and 1 strand of A, make four ch-4 button loops and attach them to left front edge, the first one above lower edge rib, the last one at beg of neck shaping, and 2 others spaced evenly between.

Sew on buttons opposite button loops.

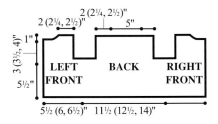

**Pretty in pink—or white, or blue— this fitted turtleneck shell is a wardrobe must. Basic stockinette stitch with full-fashioning details make this quick knit simply chic. Designed by Margery Winter.**

## SIZES

Instructions are written for size Small. Changes for Medium and Large are in parentheses.

## KNITTED MEASUREMENTS

- Waist 29½ (33, 36)"/75 (84, 91.5)cm
- Bust 34½ (38, 41)"/87.5 (96.5, 104)cm
- Length 21 (21½, 22)"/53 (54.5, 56)cm

## MATERIALS

- 7 (8, 9) 1¾oz/50g skeins (each approx 55yd/49m) of Berroco, Inc. *Pronto* (cotton/acrylic ⑤) in #4443 pink
- One pair each sizes 10 and 10½ (6 and 6.5mm) needles *or size to obtain gauge*
- Size 10 (6mm) circular needle, 16"/40 cm long

## GAUGE

13 sts and 19 rows to 4"/10cm over St st using size 10½ (mm) needles.
*Take time to check gauge.*

## BACK

With smaller needles, cast on 49 (55, 59) sts. Work in k1, p1 rib for 4 rows, dec 1 st on last row—48 (54, 58) sts. Change to larger needles and work in St st until piece measures 5½"/14cm from beg. Inc 1 st each side on next row, then every 8th row 3 times more—56 (62, 66) sts. Work even until piece measures 12½"/32cm from beg.

### Armhole shaping

**Row 1 (RS)** K2, p1, k2tog, k to last 5 sts, SKP, p1, k2.

**Rows 2 and 4** K1, p1, k1, p to last 3 sts, k1, p1, k1.

**Row 3** K2, p1, k to last 3 sts, p1, k2. Rep last 4 rows 5 (6, 7) times more—44 (48, 50) sts. Work even until armhole measures 7½ (8, 8½)"/19 (20.5, 21.5)cm.

### Shoulder shaping

Bind off 4 (5, 5) sts at beg of next 4 (4, 2) rows, 0 (0, 6) sts at beg of next 0 (0, 2) rows. Bind off rem 28 sts for back neck.

## FRONT

Work as for back until armhole measures 6 (6½, 7)"/15 (16.5, 18)cm.

### Neck shaping

**Next row (RS)** Work 13 (15, 16) sts, join a 2nd ball of yarn and bind off center 18 sts, work to end. Working both sides at once, dec 1 st at neck edge every other row 5 times. Work even until same length as back to shoulders. Shape shoulders as for back.

Block pieces to measurements. Sew shoulder and side seams.

**Neckband**

With RS facing and circular needle, pick up and k62 sts evenly around neck edge. Join and work in k1, p1 rib for 4"/10cm. Bind off.

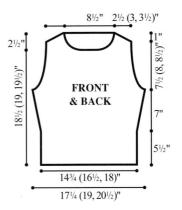

8½"   2½ (3, 3½)"

2½"

18½ (19, 19½)"

7½ (8, 8½)"

1"

**FRONT & BACK**

7"

5½"

14¾ (16½, 18)"

17¼ (19, 20½)"

# STRIPED VEST

*Chill chaser*

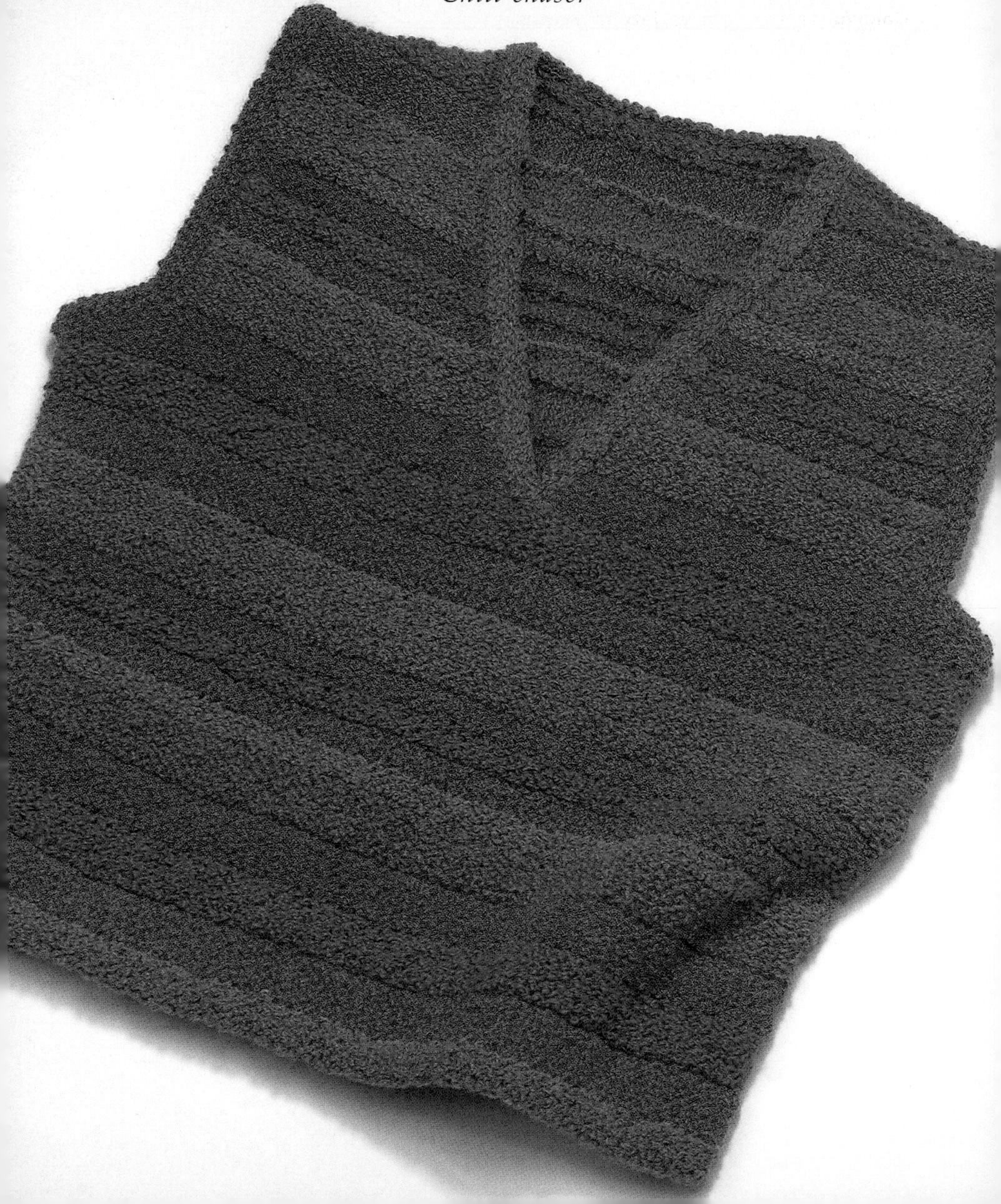

## Colorful stripes in a variety of widths jazz up this V-neck vest designed by Deborah Newton. A stockinette row at every color change makes a neat ridge between the reverse stockinette stripe.

### SIZES
Instructions are written for size Small. Changes for Medium and Large are in parentheses.

### KNITTED MEASUREMENTS
- Bust 36 (39, 42)"/91.5 (99, 106.5)cm
- Length 21 (21, 21½)"/53 (53, 54.5)cm

### MATERIALS
- 3 (3, 4) 1¾oz/50g skeins (each approx 52yd/48m) of Classic Elite Yarns *Zoom* (wool/alpaca ⑤) each in #1031 turquoise (A) and #1085 orange (B)
- 2 skeins each in #1057 blue (C), #1081 green (D) and #1019 pink (E)
- One pair size10 (6mm) needles *or size to obtain gauge*
- Size 10 (6mm) circular needle, 24"/60cm long
- Stitch marker

### GAUGE
15 sts and 26 rows to 4"/10cm over stripe pat using size 10 (6mm) needles.
*Take time to check gauge.*

### STRIPE PATTERN
With A, beg with a WS (purl) row, work in rev St st for 7 rows. *With B, work in St st for 1 row, rev St st for 6 rows; rep from * 3 times more, working 7 rows each in C, D and E. **With A, work in St st for 1 row, rev St st for 3 rows; rep from ** 4 times more, working 4 rows each in B, C, D and E. With A, work in St st for 1 row, rev St st for 6 rows.
Rep from * (55 rows) for stripe pat.

### BACK
With A, cast on 67 (73, 79) sts. Work in stripe pat for 12"/30.5cm
**Armhole shaping**
**Next row (RS)** Cont in stripe pat, bind off 2 sts at beg of next 6 (8, 10) rows—55 (57, 59) sts. Work even until armhole measures 8 (8, 8½)"/20.5 (20.5, 21.5)cm.
**Shoulder and neck and shaping**
Bind off 4 (5, 6) sts at beg of next 4 rows, 7 (6, 5) sts at beg of next 2 rows, AT SAME TIME, bind off center 9 sts, and working both sides at once, bind off 4 sts from each neck edge twice.

### FRONT
Work as for back same length as back to armhole shaping. Mark center st.
**Armhole and neck shaping**
**Next row (RS)** Work to center st, join a 2nd ball of yarn and bind off center st, work to end. Working both sides at once, shape armhole as for back, AT SAME

TIME, dec 1 st at each neck edge every 4th row 12 times—15 (16, 17) sts. Work even until piece measures same as back to shoulders. Shape shoulders as for back.

**FINISHING**

Block pieces to measurements. Sew shoulder seams.

**Armhole bands**

With RS facing and B, pick up and k76 (76, 80) sts evenly around armhole edge. K 1 row, p 1 row. Bind off knitwise. Sew side and armhole band seams.

**Neck edge**

With RS facing, circular needle and A, beg at lower V-neck and pick up and k40 (40, 42) sts along right front neck edge, 25 sts along back neck edge, 40 (40, 42) sts along left front neck edge—105 (105, 109) sts. Do not join. Work back and forth as foll: K1 row, p1 row. Bind off knitwise. Tack down ends at center front V (right over left).

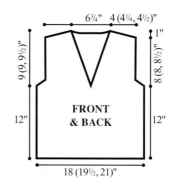

FRONT & BACK

6¾"  4 (4¼, 4½)"

1"

9 (9, 9½)"

8 (8, 8½)"

12"

12"

18 (19½, 21)"

*For Intermediate Knitters*

**The pullover he'll reach for first. This chunky classic features ribbed cuffs, hem and crewneck. Yoke and body are knit separately and joined at the chest. Diagonal and horizontal stitching create interesting pattern play. Designed by Norah Gaughan.**

SIZES

Instructions are written for Men's size Small. Changes for Medium, Large, and X-Large are in parentheses.

KNITTED MEASUREMENTS

- Chest 42 (46, 50, 54)"/106.5 (117, 127, 137)cm
- Length 26 (26½, 27, 27½)"/66 (67, 68.5, 70)cm
- Upper arm 17 (18, 19, 20)"/43 (45.5, 48, 51)cm

MATERIALS

- 10 (11, 12, 13) 3½oz/100g skeins (each approx 76yd/70m) of Artful Yarns *Museum* (wool ⑥) in #9 blue
- One pair each sizes 10½ and 13 (6.5 and 9mm) needles *or size to obtain gauge*
- Sizes 10½ and 13 (6.5 and 9mm) circular needles, 24"/60cm long
- Size 10½ (6.5mm) circular neede, 16"/40cm long

GAUGE

9 sts and 12 rows to 4"/10cm over St st

using size 13 (9mm) needles.
*Take time to check gauge.*

RIGHT SLEEVE

With smaller needles, cast on 24 (26, 28, 30) sts. Work in k1, p1 rib for 2"/5cm. Change to larger needles and work in St st until piece measures 3"/7.5cm from beg. **Next (inc) row (RS)** K2, M1, work to last 2 sts, M1, k2. Rep inc row every 6th row 4 times more, every 8th row 3 times—40 (42, 44, 46) sts. Work even until piece measures 21"/53cm from beg.

YOKE

**Next row (RS)** Cast on 10 sts, on these 10 sts work (p2, k2) twice, p2, work to end. **Next row** Cast on 10 sts, on these 10 sts work (k2, p2) twice, k2, work to last 10 sts, (k2, p2) twice, k2—60 (62, 64, 66) sts. Cont as established until piece measures 6 (7, 8, 9)"/15 (18, 20.5, 23)cm from beg of yoke (right shoulder).

**Neck shaping**

**Next row (RS)** Work 29 (30, 31, 32) sts, join a 2nd skein of yarn and bind off 2 sts, work to end. Working both sides at once, work dec row at each neck edge (at shoulders) as foll: On front, work to last 3 sts, ssk, k1; on back, k1, k2tog, work to end. Cont to work dec on front only every other row 2 times more, work even on back sts—26 (27, 28, 29) sts on front, 28 (29, 30, 31) sts on back. Work even on both sides until piece measures 6½"/16.5cm from beg of neck shaping. **Next (inc) row (RS)** Work to last st of front, M1, k1; on back, k1, M1, work to end. Rep inc row at front edge only every other row twice more—29 (30, 31, 32) sts each side. **Next row (RS)** Work to end of front, cast on 2 sts, join front and back by using same skein of yarn, work to end—60 (62, 64, 66) sts. Work even until piece measures 6 (7, 8, 9)"/15 (18, 20.5, 23)cm from end of neck shaping (left shoulder).

LEFT SLEEVE
Bind off 10 sts at beg of next 2 rows—40 (42, 44, 46) sts. Work 4 rows even. **Next (dec) row (RS)** K2, k2tog, work to last 4 sts, ssk, k2. Rep dec row every 8th row 3 times more, every 6th row 4 times—24 (26, 28, 30) sts. Work even until sleeve measures 19"/48cm. Change to smaller needles.

Work in k1, p1 rib for 2"/5cm. Bind off.Sew underarm seams and yoke extension.

**BODY**
With larger 24"/60cm circular needle, pick up and k94 (104, 114, 122) sts evenly around lower edge of yoke edge. Join and work in rnds of St st (k every rnd) until body measures 11½"/29cm. Change to smaller 24"/60cm circular needle and k1 rnd. Work in k1, p1 rib for 2"/5cm. Bind off in rib.

**BODY**
Block lightly.
**Neckband**
With RS facing and 16"/40cm circular needle, pick up and k48 sts around neck edge. Join and work in rnds of k1, p1 rib for 1"/2.5cm. Bind off in rib.

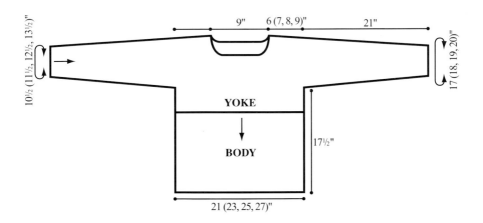

9"  6 (7, 8, 9)"  21"

10½ (11½, 12½, 13½)"  17 (18, 19, 20)"

YOKE

↓

BODY

17½"

21 (23, 25, 27)"

# NOTES

# NOTES

# NOTES

# NOTES

# RESOURCES

## US RESOURCES

*Write to the yarn companies listed below for purchasing and mail-order information.*

**ARTEMIS**
179 High Street
S.Portland, MN 04106

**ARTFUL YARNS**
distributed by
JCA

**BERROCO, INC.**
14 Elmdale Road
PO Box 367
Uxbridge, MA 01569

**BROWN SHEEP YARN CO.**
100662 County Road 16
Mitchell, NE 69357

**CHERRY TREE HILL INC.**
PO Box 659
Barton, VT 05822

**CLASSIC ELITE YARNS**
300 Jackson Street
Lowell, MA 01852

**DALE OF NORWAY**
N16 W23390 Stoneridge
Drive, Suite A
Waukesha, WI 53188

**DEBBIE BLISS YARNS**
distributed by
KFI

**DESIGNS BY JUDITH**
PO Box 770
Medford, MA 02155

**HANAH SILK**
distributed by
Artemis

**JCA**
35 Scales Lane
Townsend, MA 01469

**K1C2, LLC**
2220 Eastman Ave. #105
Ventura, CA 93003

**KFI**
35 Debevoise Ave.
Roosevelt, NY 11575

**KOIGU WOOL DESIGNS**
RR#1
Williamsford, ON N0H 2V0

**LILY®**
PO Box 40
Listowel, ON N4W3H3

**LION BRAND YARN CO.**
34 West 15th Street
New York, NY 10011

**MANOS DEL URUGUAY**
distributed by
Designs by Judith

**MISSION FALLS**
distributed by
Unique Kolours

**M&J TRIMMING**
www.mjtrim.com

**MOUNTAIN COLORS**
PO Box 156
Corvallis, MT 59828

**NATURALLY**
distributed
S.R. Kertzer, Ltd.

**REYNOLDS**
distributed by
JCA

**ROWAN YARNS**
4 Townsend West, Unit 8
Nashua, NH 03063

**S. R. KERTZER, LTD.**
105A Winges Road
Woodbridge, ON L4L 6C2
Canada

**TRENDSETTER YARN**
16745 Saticoy Street #101
Van Nuys, CA 91406

**UNIQUE KOLOURS**
1428 Oak Lane
Downingtown, PA 19335

**WENDY**
distributed by
Berroco, Inc.

## CANADIAN RESOURCES

*Write to US resources for mail-order availability of yarns not listed.*

**BERROCO, INC.**
distributed by
S. R. Kertzer, Ltd.

**CLASSIC ELITE YARNS**
distributed by
S. R. Kertzer, Ltd.

**DIAMOND YARN**
9697 St. Laurent
Montreal, PQ H3L 2N1
and
155 Martin Ross, Unit #3
Toronto, ON M3J 2L9

**KOIGU WOOL DESIGNS**
RR#1
Williamsford, ON N0H 2V0

**LILY®**
PO Box 40
Listowel, ON N4W3H3

**MISSION FALLS**
PO Box 224
Consecon, ON K0K 1T0

**PATONS®**
PO Box 40
Listowel, ON N4W 3H3

**ROWAN YARNS**
distributed by
Diamond Yarn

**S. R. KERTZER, LTD.**
105A Winges Rd.
Woodbridge, ON L4L 6C2

---

## UK RESOURCES

*Not all yarns used in this book are available in the UK. For yarns not available, make a comparable substitute or contact the US manufacturer for purchasing and mail-order information.*

**SILKSTONE**
12 Market Place
Cockermouth
Cumbria, CA13 9NQ
Tel: 01900-821052

**THOMAS RAMSDEN GROUP**
Netherfield Road
Guiseley
West Yorks LS20 9PD
Tel: 01943-872264

# VOGUE KNITTING WEEKEND KNITS

Editor-in-Chief
**TRISHA MALCOLM**

Art Director
**CHI LING MOY**

Executive Editor
**CARLA S. SCOTT**

Instructions Editor
**KAREN GREENWALD**

Knitting Editor
**JEAN GUIRGUIS**

Yarn Editor
**VERONICA MANNO**

Editorial Coordinator
**MICHELLE LO**

Photography
**EYE[4]MEDIA**

Book Managers
**THERESA MCKEON**
**CARA BECKERICH**

Production Manager
**DAVID JOINNIDES**

President, Sixth&Spring Books
**ART JOINNIDES**

## LOOK FOR THESE OTHER TITLES IN
## *THE VOGUE KNITTING ON THE GO SERIES...*